Leftovers & Heartfelt Letters

A collection of poems that are not about love

Sheila Curiel

BookLeaf Publishing

India | USA | UK

Made with ❤ on the BookLeaf Publishing Platform
www.bookleafpub.in
www.bookleafpub.com

Dedication

I wrote this for you, because you meant a lot.
And I said I would.

Preface

These poems are fragments of love, loss, and the unanswered questions that linger in the quietest moments. They hold the weight of fleeting connections, raw emotions, and the restless search for meaning.

Acknowledgements

To you, the inspiration of years.

The poems you never saw.

1. Let's Start With The End

You're slipping away,
You're in the reflection that catches frames
When I am at the edge and the train is about to arrive.

I've had only thanks to say to you,
Lovely soul that's not mine.
Thank you so much,
But I'm yours, and you are not mine.

I will stay in orange seats and metal strings,
Remembering this last train ride with you.
Cold middle of November,
Those playing their music behind us created echoes.

I'll miss this last train ride with you.
I've never seen such brown eyes,
Capturing the essence of a child,
Making me feel loved.

I'll miss these train rides with you forever,
Reading wall-posted poetry,
Seeing first lovers be.

I'll miss these train rides with you,

Alongside the bridge where I thought
You and I would make history.

No goodbye kiss,
No hug,
No shivering hands holding on,
No looks back while walking away.

Only strong steps against concrete
And blowing scarves,
Echoing voices,
And a playlist to cry on my way back home
Without you.

How pathetic.

2. The Accident of You

Do you light a fire inside of you to feel warmth
Or to fill a lonely void?

The smoke that comes out while you exhale—
Do you see the shapes of angels or demons?

At night, when you sleep and your thoughts
Are too loud, do you light up that fire?
The one that feeds your soul or the one that numbs your
mind?

I'm just curious to know,
To know about you,
But cautious enough
Not to share a full night with you.

I think you have a mind I could pick on all day
And comfort at night.

Let me take your thoughts
And turn them into clouds.

3. Galus

I don't like you that much.
You make it hard to stay away,
And for that reason,
You need to leave me alone
And never come back to me.
Or...
Are you meant to find your way back through a sin?
I don't want to smile
When I hear your voice.
Neither do I want my skin to shiver
When I see you coming near.
I do not desire
To have you next to me.

4. December

Do you also close your eyes
And imagine the scenes and the dialogues?
The silent, shaky camera effect
While you run desperately on a cold night for your life.
Seeing the smoke coming out of your mouth,
The moon following you.

An insert shot.
A close-up of your eyes.
And there you have a million flashbacks
To all those moments you thought forgotten.
It brings you back in a spiral,
A domino effect of memories.
I hate that you inspire me

To the point of death.

5. Lucky Winners!

You will
Forget about me
Eventually.

The memory of my laugh will fade from your mind,
And one day, you'll come across something that reminds
you of me.
You will smile just enough to sigh,
Then go back to your day.

I'll never see you again.
I miss you, but it's okay.
We must let it go.
The destiny we've been given is beyond us —
Like the man outside the liquor store,
Scratching a lottery ticket with dirt under his nails.

6. Bitul

All of me, I gave in.
Unconditional nullification.
No one saw it coming.
The biggest sacrifice was giving in—
Into something bigger
Than me,
Than you,
Than us.
Nothing is left but to take refuge in fantasy.
I saw you coming, with no doubt in mind.
All we did was right.
Right steps,
Right timing.
It was just all above us.

7. 1580

I don't have the words to fancy your eyes,
And maybe I won't have what it takes to make you want
to stay.

The truth is, there is no answer for us.
We are an unresolved midnight thought.

But not for their sake — for our sake —
Can we just take it all in and make a space?

It's all beautiful — you and me,
In hidden walls between President and Troy,
Midnight bodega runs to pick up the substance
That will allow us to forget who we are
And all the reasons why we can't be.
But none of them matter,
And we couldn't care less.

I don't think you understand my extent.
There is always one who loves more,
And I am the one who loves more —
But you will never know that.

8. Letters In A Soup

I feel surrounded by these words and feelings,
And I can't seem to bring them all together,
Like letters in a soup.
I feel powerless and hopeless.
I want to be hopeful.
I want you — but do I really need you?
I wanted to fight for us,
But I was the one to let go
When our days came to an end.

9. Reset

From which places did we both escape?
From where we both tried to render our minds,
To reset our destinies.
We were nullified.
And in the end, the questions embarked,
And we asked:
Do we? Can we?
There's no option,
No way to turn and go.
There's nothing we could have done,
Nothing we could do.
And that was our end.
That was our beginning.
And the rebirth of my faith.
You will find another to tell your secrets to.
I am glad I never bought those plants.
Hanging them like air roots in a garden
Would have made it more painful for me to walk away.

10. Man of Words

The birds stopped singing at our window.
The flowers ran out of water.
You kiss me slowly, and you drift.

I wrote about you.
I wrote about you in every single chapter,
Every sentence,
Every word.

And when you run your fingers through the pages,
I hope you feel as if you are running your fingers
through my hair.

11. With You

I'm deep in high waters,
And I am the one in command —
Shifting my boat toward deeper waters,
Rather than searching for land.

12. Over and Over

My heart, holding on for dear life.
I'm at my last chance.
I have one last breath to give — if I don't find you now,
I will lose.
Our last morning started like any other before.
I didn't think it through.
I wanted to cry, to tell you:
"Don't let me go."
And then I remembered —
I don't want to be with you anymore.

13. Leather Grey Shoes and Old Coat

Sitting in overpriced Uber rides,
Making small talk about the heater settings.
Traveling back and forth on the same streets every day
—

Seeing the same woman carrying her bags.
A routine.
She's wearing a different color beanie today.
She doesn't know I notice.
I wonder if you thought about me today.

14. Offering

15

My spiritualism is numbed
I saw red brick station and you were there static
Making an offering

15. Today

I missed you.
I wanted to call you,
And I almost did.
I almost forgot.
I was filled with excitement,
Rounding up in my head all the things I'd done —
All the amazing places I visited,
All the stories I wanted to tell you.
All of it.
And then it hit me —
I would never have that again.
At least not with you.
And my heart broke.
A little.
I swallowed hard and held my grip.
At least I think I did.
Held it together —
Together enough to fall asleep.
Then I woke up.
And had to do it all over again.
Today.
Today, I almost called you.

16. The Come Back

It's so interesting how it's not about you anymore.
The city and the stations I stop in,
The street corners I pass with flowers —
It's not your city.
It never was.
I just made it yours.
And now I'm coming back as a newcomer.
Everything was about to change,
And I felt it on the 4 train.
There's nothing you can take from me anymore.
I see you, and your source is all good.
You are pure holiness.
That's what I always saw in you,
What drew me close.
But your light was never mine to discover.
And that's what I had to learn.

17. Brown Eyes

I looked at him from my side,
And as our eyes met, he said to me,
"It hurts. You're so beautiful, it hurts."
I didn't understand what he meant by that.
Now I know.
For him, it meant he knew I wasn't his,
And it would hurt —
How much we would just never be.

18. The Dream

19

I dreamt of you last night,
And now I'm having breakfast with the love of my life.
And still, I think of you.

If you weren't the love of my life,
Then what were you?

19. Mystical Energy

I cried and wrote about you last night.
I screamed your name to the heavens, asking for
answers.

Today, you showed me the same side of you.
Am I sick? Addicted? Or is it simply the truth—
That we are both bonded beyond ourselves,
Through mystical energy.

20. Game Over

When I speak to you, my body trembles.
When I hear your voice, I crash and fall.

As much as I love the rush you give me—

Like a drug—
You are not good for me.

And I'm scared that I love you too much.
Your love was always conditional,
And you were the only winner.

21. Congratulations

We fall in love—
Truly, deeply.
And yet, we crave love
That isn't meant for us,
Love that isn't healthy.
We condition ourselves to crave it.
It hurts.
It breaks us.
It leaves us with nothing.
We leave, and we come back.
Why?
I don't really know.
What I can tell you for certain is this:
True love will be what you least expect,
And when it finds you, you'll know.
Maybe you already do.

I do,
And it wasn't you.